The Truth About Annuities

The Simple Survivor's Guide

By Tony J. Hansmann

The Truth About Annuities: The Simple Survivors Guide

Printed in the United States of America

First Printing, 2017

ISBN 978-1548139551

Cover Design & Interior Layout: Wesley Useche

Acknowledgment

Dedicated to my Family and Friends.

Table of Contents

Introduction 7

1 – Type of Annuities 11

2 – What is the Purpose of an Annuity 23

3 - Features of Annuities 37

4 – Understanding Annuity Fee Structures . . . 49

5 – Pros and Cons of Annuities 60

6 – Why Brokers Like Variable Annuities. 78

7 – Why You Should Only Work With a
Fiduciary Financial Advisor. 88

Summary. 97

Introduction

It's not uncommon for working people in the United States to put all of their time and energy into building a career they can be proud of. Some of them earn college degrees and some do not, but they all want to be successful.

There's nothing wrong with that approach except this: it doesn't go far enough. For too many people, career planning takes center stage while retirement planning gets pushed to the side.

The problem with that, of course, is that retirement can end up being impossible for people who haven't planned properly. They don't know what they need financially and, because they haven't thought about it and planned for it, they end up falling short of what they need.

That's where I come in. I've been working as a Financial Planner for more than 20 years and I help people prepare for retirement all the time. I know how to assess my clients' financial needs, help them to maximize their Social Security benefits, and how to make smart investments that will provide them with the steady, predictable income they need to retire peacefully.

After writing my last book about Social Security, I knew I wanted to branch out. It's easy to make mistakes when investing for retirement and choosing the right investments is important.

The Importance of Preparing Financially for Retirement
People who already have a 401K or an IRA or a pension often think that they don't need to do any additional planning or preparation for retirement.

I never like to hear that because I think it's very easy to get complacent about retirement. The truth is that there are a lot of variables that can affect your ability to retire and if you ignore them, you may end up finding that you simply don't have enough money to live on.

It's not enough to open one retirement account and hope for the best. If you do that, what will you do if there's a big stock market crash or a bank failure?

Even if you don't fall victim to a market downturn or something of that nature, there's still the issue of longevity to consider. People are living longer now than ever before. If you retire at the age of 66 or 70, will you have enough money to last until you're 90 or 95? What about your spouse?

This isn't meant to scare you, but rather, to make you think. I tell my clients that the single most important thing they can do is to prepare for retirement starting as early as possible. I wish I could get every client when they're fresh out of college and working their first job so they would have the maximum amount of time to prepare for retirement. One of the tools I sometimes recommend to my clients is investing in the right type of annuity. Annuities provide you with a reliable source of income and are an extremely effective way to supplement your Social Security income.

The purpose of this book is to help you understand the different types of annuities and how they work. When you understand their purpose, then you can see why I might recommend them as a good way to plan for retirement.

I'll explain what your options are when you buy an annuity, and the specific features of annuities that you may want to consider, including death benefits, tax deferral, and annuitization.

I'll also tell you how the fee structures of annuities work because they can vary from type to type. I'll share what I think are the pros and cons of buying an annuity, and then, I'll explain why brokers like annuities.

Finally, to close out the book, I'll give you my take on why you should work only with a fiduciary financial advisor as you plan for retirement.

Working with a fiduciary ensures that you will have capable, experienced, and rational advice to help you prepare for the realities of retirement using the resources you have.

By the time you have finished reading, you will know everything you need to know about annuities – and you'll be ready to make a decision about whether investing in one is right for you

To Your Continued Success,

Tony J. Hansmann

Chapter 1
Type of Annuities

Any discussion about why annuities are a good investment choice for those preparing for retirement must begin with a review of the types of annuities available. As is the case with any investment, you have multiple options to consider.

The choices you make now will have a profound impact in your ability to retire without stress and enjoy your post-work life. Yet, research shows that one in three Americans have no retirement savings at all.[1] The fact that you are reading this book shows that you want to make preparations, and learning about annuities is a good place to start.

In this chapter, I will explain fixed income annuities, variable annuities, and the differences between immediate and deferred annuities. I'll briefly discuss other annuity options, including equity-indexed annuities and longevity annuities. I'll also talk some of the variables to keep in mind, including single versus multi-owner annuities.

What is a Fixed Income Annuity?
As its name suggests, a fixed income annuity is a form of investment that offers a guaranteed annual payout. It is a predictable and conservative investment that can serve as a supplement to Social Security or a pension plan.[2]

A fixed income annuity has some things in common with a traditional IRA or a 401K plan in that, at least in some cases, it allows you to defer paying taxes on your investments until you withdraw money. That can be a real benefit to some people, particularly those who can use investments to move themselves into a lower tax bracket.

The basic features of a fixed income annuity are as follows:

1. You make a lump sum payment to an insurance company in return for receiving fixed annual payments at a future date. The date when you can begin to withdraw money may vary from plan to plan, but the basic idea is the same.

2. Fixed income annuities guarantee a particular interest rate, so you are guaranteed a modest return on your investment regardless of what happens with the economy or interest rates. The income rate is usually a conservative one, and that's what enables the insurance company to provide fixed income annuities as an option for their clients.

3. The annuity provides you with guaranteed income for the duration of your life. In some cases, it may also provide your spouse with guaranteed income if you die first.

For some people, having the ability to control the payouts they receive each year provides real peace of mind. They can perhaps afford to be aggressive with other investment decisions when they know that they won't be without income for retirement.

What is a Variable Annuity?

Variable annuities differ from fixed income annuities in one key way. Like fixed income annuities, they offer annual payments that you can use to supplement income from Social Security or a pension.

Unlike fixed income annuities, variable annuities offer returns that are tied to the performance of the investments you choose. They offer more flexibility than fixed income annuities, but they also come with more risk.[3]

People who choose to invest in a variable annuity have the option of investing in professionally managed accounts in a variety of asset classes. The choices may include stocks, bonds, money market accounts, and other investment options.

By investing in these subaccounts, the owner of the variable annuity has the chance to earn higher annual payments than would be possible with a fixed income annuity. If their investments outperform the market in general, then they may be able to increase their annual payments and earn more income than they would be able to with a fixed annuity.

Of course, the reverse is true, too. If their investments do poorly, then they run the risk of receiving lower than expected payments, and that can have an impact on their ability to retire and on the comfort of their lives once they do retire.

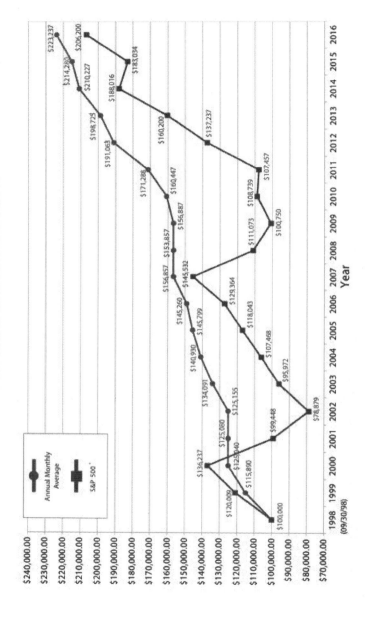

Average Return of a Fixed Annuity From 1998 to 2016

*This graph is based on actual credited rates for the period shown. The actual Participation Rates for this time period, applied to the calculation as depicted, vary between 50% and 70%, and a Minimum Guaranteed Contract Value of 3% is assumed. The S&P 500 is an annual point to point calculation depicting the actual change in the index year over year.
Past performance is not an indication of future results.

The benefit of investing in an annuity is that it provides you with income security. Variable annuities do not do as good a job of that as fixed income annuities because of the uncertainty that's inherent in their structure. If you choose investments wisely (and have some luck), you might do very well with a variable annuity – but you have to be willing to tolerate the risk associated with them.

It may help you understand variable annuities if you know that they are sometimes referred to as "mutual funds with an insurance wrapper."[4] They offer some of the benefits of mutual funds, but you obtain them through an insurance company.

The other primary difference between a fixed income annuity and a variable annuity is that some variable annuities guarantee that, if you die, your heirs will receive the balance of your initial investment. Variable annuities recalculate the amount left in the account and recalculate the guaranteed income, which in some cases may be significantly smaller than what the account holder collected.

What is a Fixed Index Annuity?
In many ways, a fixed index annuity is a hybrid of a fixed annuity and a variable annuity.[5] However, for the most part it is a variation on a fixed annuity.

These annuities offer a minimum guaranteed monthly payment in the same way that traditional fixed income annuities do. However, they also offer the chance to earn a higher return by using a formula that's tied to the performance of a particular stock market index. (The S & P 500 is an example of a popular stock market index.)

Fixed index annuities have some significant benefits. The money you earn is tied to the index you choose. You can earn more when the index performs well, and you also have the risk of earning less when it performs poorly. There is typically a limit on the amount that will be paid to you when the index is up, and that's to protect the annuity holder at times when the index is down.

All annuities typically specify the penalties that will be charged if you withdraw money early, close your account, or transfer it to another financial institution. These are known as surrender charges.[6] The surrender charges are there to protect the insurance company.

Fixed Annuity Index
$100,000 Investment

YEAR	Rate of Return	Stock Market	ANNUITY	GUARANTEE RIDER
1	9.62%	$90,380	$100,000	$107,200
2	6.97%	$96,679	$105,220	$114,918
3	7.79%	$104,210	$111,364	$123,192
4	6.72%	$97,208	$111,364	$132,062
5	0.78%	$96,450	$111,364	$141,570
6	3.12%	$99,459	$113,969	$151,763
7	6.58%	$106,003	$119,587	$162,690
8	9.60%	$95,827	$119,587	$174,404
9	17.31%	$79,240	$119,587	$186,961
10	15.76%	$91,28	$133,722	$200,423

Immediate vs. Deferred Annuities

Now that you understand the three basic types of annuities, fixed income, fixed index, and variable, let's talk about some of the variations on them. The first and most important is choosing between an immediate and a deferred annuity. Each has its benefits and risks and it's important for you to understand them before you make any decision about whether an annuity is right for you.

Immediate Annuities

I want to start with immediate annuities because they appeal to many retirees as a way of securing their money and guaranteeing a specific monthly income for the duration of their lives.

An immediate annuity is an annuity that starts to issue payments almost as soon as you create it, usually within a year.[7] The money you put in comes from post-tax dollars. You annuitize the payments, working with the insurance company to determine what your monthly payments will be based on two things:

1. The dollar amount you put into the annuity fund; and
2. The interest rate the insurance company is willing to guarantee.

It may be helpful to look at an example to see how they work.

Imagine that a man who is 60 years old has $250,000 he wants to put into an annuity. After talking to the insurance company, they set up annuitized payments that will guarantee him $1,000 per month every month for the rest of his life.

Once he makes the decision to set up an immediate, fixed annuity, he is locked into that payment amount. The money is there for him to use in his lifetime. Because he put $250,000 into the account, he would need to collect the annuity for 250 months – that's almost 21 years – to break even. That's a consideration to keep in mind.

Insurance companies do take the investor's life expectancy into consideration when determining annuity amounts. Nobody can predict mortality with 100% accuracy, but actuarial tables allow insurers to make an educated guess about how long you will need the money.

The immediate annuity is fixed, and that means that if the man dies, his family won't get the income that remains in the account. It is there solely for his use. (There is an option that continues spousal payments, and I'll explain that later in the chapter.)

The primary benefit of an immediate annuity is that it protects the money that's in the account. It doesn't matter what happens with interest rates or investments. The $1,000 will come to him every month regardless of market fluctuations.

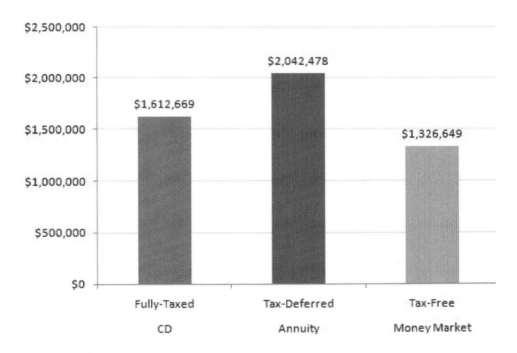

Deferred-Tax Annuities

The second option is a deferred-tax annuity. A deferred-tax annuity may be opened at any age. You may open the account with a lump sum. If you choose the fixed income annuity option, you'll get payments according to a structure similar to what I outlined above for the immediate annuity.[8]

Where deferred-tax annuities differ is if you choose the fixed index or variable option. You will still open the account with a lump sum, but then your available funds may shrink or grow depending upon the performance of your chosen investments.

If you choose a deferred-tax variable annuity, in many cases you may have the option of turning it into an immediate annuity after a certain amount of time has passed. The time required can vary from insurer to insurer so make sure to check if having this option is important to you.

Other Variables and Options
To close out this chapter and prepare you for the rest of what you will learn in this book, let's look at some of the other options and variables that you may want to consider if you buy an annuity.

Longevity Annuity
If you expect to live a long life or want some reassurance that you'll have enough money if you live past the age of 85, then you may want to consider a longevity annuity.

A longevity annuity is a type of annuity that is sometimes referred to as long life expectancy insurance.[9] Typically, the payments are deferred until you reach the age of 85, at which point you will receive a guaranteed monthly payment for the duration of your life.

These payments may be particularly helpful if people in your family tend to live to be over 100. Long life expectancies are becoming increasingly common with medical advances and it's worth considering what you will do if you end up living a very long life.

One benefit of a longevity annuity is that it can free you up to spend other income between your retirement and the age of 85 because you can be certain that you have the annuity payment to see you through.

Single Owner vs. Multi-Owner Annuities
Earlier, I mentioned that certain kinds of annuities cease making payments upon the owner's death and the heirs cannot recover even the initial investment made in the fund.

That might be discouraging to read, but now let's examine one of the options that provides financial security for both you and your spouse. It's called a joint-and-survivor benefit.[10]

Basically, the joint-and-survivor benefit makes payments to you and your spouse while you are both alive, and to the surviving spouse when one of you dies. As a rule, the monthly payments for this type of annuity are lower than they would be for a single-life annuity because the payments may last a longer time if you predecease your spouse.

The primary decision you need to make is whether you can afford to receive the lower monthly payment during your lifetime. Once you choose a structure for your annuity you won't be able to change it. However, if you have limited retirement savings and want to make sure that you provide for your spouse, then a joint-and-survivor benefit is a good option.

Annuities have other features that might factor into your decision, but we will cover those in a later chapter. The key things to remember as we move forward are:

- Fixed income annuities offer guaranteed income for the duration of your life and are a good way to supplement Social Security and pension income.

- Variable annuities offer a way to get a higher return on your initial investment than fixed income annuities, but they also carry some risk.

- Fixed index annuities are linked to the performance of a stock market index such as the S & P 500. You can receive a portion of the gain, with no downside risk.

- Immediate annuities begin giving payments right away, usually within a year of the annuity being created.

- Tax-deferred annuities may be set up in advance and you can convert them to immediate annuities if need be.

- Joint-and-survivor annuities offer protection to your spouse in the event you predecease them.

The annuity type you choose will depend upon a variety of factors, including:

- The amount of money you have to invest
- What other sources of retirement income you have, including Social Security, IRAs, 401K accounts, and pension accounts.
- Whether you are married.
- Your life expectancy.

If you work with a financial advisor, that person can help you to sort through the available options and make the best possible decision for your future.

Now that you understand the types of annuities that are available, the next chapter is where I'll explain the primary purpose of creating an annuity and why and how they can help you plan for a happy and secure retirement.

Chapter 2
What is the Purpose of an Annuity

When you think ahead to retirement, what are the things that most concern you? You've worked your whole life to be able to stop working at some point – to enjoy what some people refer to as your golden years.

One of the things that I emphasize when I talk to my clients is that the golden years are only golden if you prepare for them. In my first book, 7 Paths to Social Security Maximization - I lay out how you pay into Social Security for your entire working life, but when you take a look at what your benefits will be when you retire, they are (for many people) not enough to live on.

What that means in practical terms is that you must do whatever you can to ensure that you have sufficient income to retire. For people who are in their 40s or 50s now, that's an especially scary prospect if they haven't done any prior planning.

Let's talk about some of the reasons why annuities were created, and why guaranteed income is a must for anybody who wants to be able to retire.

Why Annuities Were Created

The original purpose of annuity payments was to provide a source of income for people who could no longer work. People who are reasonably young and in reasonably good health are able to work for a living, but people who are elderly or ill may not be able to do so.

In such cases, clearly it is in the interest of both the individual person and the general public to allow people to set up a source of income that they can rely on when it is no longer possible or desirable to work.

It may be helpful to look at some highlights from the history of annuities to understand why they were created and what the original intention of annuities was.[12]

As far back as the 1600s, some governments in Europe used annuity-like financial arrangements to subsidize public works and other projects. The very earliest individual annuities were called tontines. They provided guaranteed income during the annuity owner's life and then actually increased benefits after the owner died to provide for their dependents.

In the next century, it became somewhat common for wealthy Europeans to use annuities as a way of offsetting financial risks they took in other areas. The annuity structure allowed them to hedge against riskier investments so that they wouldn't be left with nothing in the event that another investment failed.

The first annuities in the United States actually date back to before the Revolutionary War. Pastors in Pennsylvania received lifetime payments in retirement. And by 1776, the year the Revolution started, the Continental Congress passed a resolution to provide lifetime guaranteed payments to the people who fought the British.

By 1812, commercial annuities were available to the general public. At the same time, Andrew Carnegie set up the first teacher's annuity pension, a system that is still in place today – albeit under a different name.

Over the years, various changes have been made to the way we buy and use annuities.[13] For example:

- After the Great Depression, some investors turned to annuities as a sort of safe haven from the volatility of the stock market – a strategy that still works today.

- The first deferred variable annuity was introduced in 1952, something that opened up additional options (and risks) to investors.

- In 1986, Congress passed a law that allowed investors to defer tax payments on annuity investments and benefit from tax-deferred growth on their initial investment.

- The first fixed index annuities were introduced in 1995 as an investment alternative to traditional fixed income annuities and variable annuities.
- MetLife offered the first longevity annuity in 2005, something that makes a great deal of sense,

considering increases in life expectancy and the likelihood that people will outlive their retirement savings.

As you can see, the annuities available have changed and evolved over the years. Some annuities are government payments, such as the teacher's annuity and the program created to benefit soldiers of the Revolutionary War. Others are private and meant to be used as investment tools for private citizens.

However, what they all have in common is the intention of providing a steady and guaranteed source of income to people for their retirement. That's the reason that I recommend annuities to my clients and think you might consider investing in an annuity,y too.

It makes sense for certain people who serve the country to receive annuity payments. Many pension plans arose from the desire to attempt to repay patriotic service with financial support and some degree of comfort and stability.

However, the government does not – and realistically cannot – provide guaranteed income to everybody, at least not the way it is currently structured. The demands of maintaining infrastructure, paying for national defense, and providing relief to those who need it most through programs like Medicaid is already a strain on government resources.

In practical terms, that means that anybody who wants to be sure that they can retire needs to look at investment options to supplement their Social Security income and provide them with the financial security they need to be able to retire.

The Big Three

GROWTH   SAFETY   LIQUIDITY

You Pick TWO!

Of course – we want all three, but life doesn't work that way!

Most Retirees find that Growth and Safety are the most important.

That means giving up some liquidity, but that's ok because your core retirement doesn't need liquidity.

Why Guaranteed Income is Essential for a Healthy Retirement

With some of my clients, the biggest challenge I face is getting them to understand the need for guaranteed income when they retire. It can be tricky to explain the need for an annuity to someone who hasn't really stopped to consider how expensive it will be to retire – and what they will need to be able to do so.

The thing to remember is that you need to crunch the numbers to get a true picture of what your retirement will look like. For example, do you know what you can expect to get from Social Security? Does your spouse?

Some people may end up doing better if they draw a spousal benefit under Social Security rather than collecting their own benefit. For example, a woman who worked before she had children and then quit her job to be a stay-at-home mom might have a significantly lower individual benefit than her spouse.

It's also important to look at other sources of guaranteed income – and to keep in mind that accounts tied to investments, particularly investments in the stock market, may not be "guaranteed" in the sense that it may be difficult to predict how much you can get from them.

So the first thing you need to do is to figure out how much money you will need for your retirement.[14] Let's look at some of the spending categories that you should keep in mind as you prepare.

Housing
The first and arguably the largest expense that you need to consider is housing. If you own your home outright and have no mortgage, then you don't need to worry about mortgage payments. However, you do need to think about the other expenses associated with owning a home.

Here is a list of some of the things to include in your housing costs:

- **The mortgage(s) on your home, if you have one or more.**

- **Rent on your apartment.**

- **Property taxes on any property that you own – keeping in mind that the property taxes may fluctuate with the value of your property or with changes in the tax code.**

- **Condominium fees or homeowners' association fees.**

It's important to build a bit of extra money into what you anticipate your housing costs will be to cover rises in your property tax and other unforeseen expenses.

I also want to mention here that you are under no obligation to keep going with the housing costs and obligations you have now. Many people decide to "right size" their living situation as they prepare to retire, and that's a good way to keep your housing costs under control.

For example, say that you own a large home with five bedrooms because you and your spouse had three children and wanted a guest room as well. Once all of your children are grown and out of the house, it's a good idea to ask some questions about your living arrangements. For example:

- **Do we really need all of this space for just the two of us?**

- **Are we paying more in mortgage/rent/property taxes than we need to be paying?**

■ **Do we have the physical capability to handle the upkeep on a large home and if not, can we afford to pay one or more people to help us with cleaning and yard work?**

The answers to these questions can help you determine whether it makes sense to sell a large home and look for a smaller one. The lower your housing costs are, the farther you can make your monthly income stretch.

Utilities
The next category to consider is your utility payments. It should come as no surprise that expenses for things like electricity, gas, oil, and water will be higher for a large property than they will for a small one.
You should also think about expenses that are related to utilities, such as upkeep on your furnace and fluctuations in heating prices. During times of shortage and political unrest, oil may be much more expensive than it is in times of peace and prosperity.

When you consider your utility payments, make sure to average them out for an entire year. People who live in the Northeast, for example, might pay far higher monthly utilities during the cold winter months, while for people who live in Arizona, the highest expenditures happen when the mercury soars and the air conditioner is running 24 hours a day.

Food
The next thing to consider is your outlay for food and supplies each month. Here again, you want to look at

averages. Track your grocery bills over a period of several months or even a year to get an idea of how much you spend.

This is another area where you might benefit from some right sizing. For example, a person who is in the habit of buying expensive gourmet food on a regular basis might be able to reduce spending by saving those splurges for special occasions. If you don't want to make those cuts, then you'll have to make sure that your guaranteed income is sufficient to cover the lifestyle you want to live.

Clothing

Some people may find that they need fewer clothing options after retirement because they don't need to invest in suits and formal attire (or at least, not as much as they used to.)

However, you still have to buy clothes on a regular basis. You'll need shoes, too, and it's important to make sure that the guaranteed income you collect is sufficient to cover most (if not all) routine expenditures for clothing and apparel.

Insurance

There's no question that insurance is of paramount concern to anybody who wants to retire, and you have multiple kinds of insurance to take into consideration.

First, you need to think about the continuation of insurance that you already pay for. That includes things like:

- **Homeowner's insurance**

- **Automobile insurance**
- **Life insurance**
- **Long-term care insurance**
- **Pet insurance**

However, you also need to consider forms of insurance that you might not need now but will need later on. I'm talking, of course, about Medicare supplement insurance.

Many people, in my experience, underestimate how much they will have to pay for supplemental health insurance and prescription drug insurance. They don't really understand how early in the year they can max out their prescription drug benefit, for example, and fall into the Medicare "donut hole" where they have to cover those expenses out of pocket.

Keep in mind that even if you are in relatively good health now, you might end up having to take a lot of maintenance medications as you get older. Some examples of maintenance medications include medication for your blood pressure or for diabetes.

You can't predict how much you will have to pay for supplemental insurance, but you do need to make sure that you have enough guaranteed income to cover your present insurance needs plus enough to cover most – if not all – of any additional insurance you might need going forward.

It's also important to keep out of pocket expenses in mind. With Medicare, you probably won't be on the hook for all of the expenses associated with a surgery or hospital stay, but you will have to come up with your deductible and pay up to your out-of-pocket maximum.

Entertainment

It might be tempting to leave entertainment out of the equation when the time comes to calculate what you need in guaranteed income, but it's important to make an estimate and build it into your budget.

It's true that you might not go out as much as you did when you were working, but some people go out more often. They relish the thought of having a full and interesting social life without the strictures of work.

The best way to approach your entertainment budget is to keep track of what you spend now and then ask yourself what you think you will spend in retirement. For example, if you eat out once a week now and you want to continue that practice in retirement, you need to build that into your entertainment budget.

The same is true of other entertainment expenses, including:

- **Movie tickets**
- **Theater tickets**
- **Concert tickets**
- **Sporting events**
- **Community events like festivals, fairs, wine tastings, and so on.**

It is, of course, perfectly acceptable to right size here too –
but be realistic. You're not going to want to be stuck at home
all the time and getting out of the house and doing fun
things is important.

Travel
Many people make big travel plans for their retirement.
They vow that they will finally make a comprehensive tour
of Europe, visit Machu Picchu, or take an annual Caribbean
cruise.

You should absolutely make sure to build vacation expenses
into your budget for retirement – and don't forget to include
weekend trips to visit your grandchildren or friends.

Travel expenses need to include everything, including:

- **Airfare**
- **Hotel**
- **Car rental**
- **Meals**
- **Tips**
- **Entertainment**

Of course you don't have to break the bank every time you
travel, and you'll have to balance the comforts and amenities
you want against what you can realistically afford to spend.

Incidental Expenses

Finally, one of the biggest and most unpredictable things you should be considering as you prepare for retirement are the incidental expenses that may arise as you age.

This category covers many things, including:

- **Maintenance and replacement of large and small appliances**
- **Yard care and landscaping**
- **Automobile repairs and maintenance**
- **Travel emergencies**
- **Any other unexpected expenses**

I don't tell you this to frighten you, but rather to help you understand the importance of having guaranteed income that you can count on. You might have a very nice nest egg, but what will you do if you have to dip into it repeatedly to cover unexpected expenses?

You need to consider what you expect to receive alongside any other forms of guaranteed payment you might have. It's also important to consider whether your pension payments, for example, might affect what you can expect to get from Social Security – something I covered extensively in my last book.

The bottom line is that having guaranteed income does all of the following:

1. It helps ensure that you have the regular income – whether you collect it on a monthly, quarterly, or

annual basis – to cover your regular living expenses, including your mortgage or rent, property taxes, utility, food, clothing, insurance, and entertainment expenses.

2. Provides you with a cushion so that if you do have to dip into your nest egg to pay for unexpected or incidental expenses, you can be confident that you're not going to be putting yourself into a difficult position down the line.

3. Removes the possibility that your children or grandchildren will feel obligated to support you during your retirement.

4. Makes it possible to preserve as much of your nest egg as possible so you can leave it to your children and other heirs if it is important for you to be able to do so.

Most importantly, having one or more regular sources of guaranteed income ensures that you will be able to enjoy your retirement. Many of the people I advise are fearful about retirement. They want to be able to enjoy the fruits of their labor and worry that they will not be able to do so.

The primary benefit of investing in an annuity is that it removes much of that worry from the table. It makes it possible for you to retire and feel confident that you will have the money you need to pay your regular expenses.

Annuities make a lot of sense, but the key here is to pick the right kind of annuity. To do that, you must understand the features of annuities and how they work – and that's what we'll cover in the next chapter.

Chapter 3
Features of Annuities

The features that are most commonly associated with annuities are also often misunderstood.

The benefits and features built into annuities all come with fees attached. We'll talk more about that later, but the other thing that you need to know is that the language in annuities is very much like the language in any legal documents. It can be very confusing.

That being the case, you absolutely must take the time to understand the way that the features of any annuity you are considering work. You need to understand them thoroughly to avoid making the kind of costly mistake that could eat into your initial investment and cost you money – sometimes a lot of money – in the long term.

Death Benefits

Let's start by talking about the death benefit, one of the most popular features that you can elect when buying an annuity.

It's understandable for investors to want a death benefit. As I mentioned earlier, it used to be common for heirs to forfeit any capital left in an annuity fund after the owner of the fund died. Now it is easier for your survivors to withdraw money. However, you must take the time to understand how the death benefit works so you don't actually end up worse off than you would have been if you hadn't bought it.

The typical death benefit works like this:[15]

1. You make an initial investment in your annuity, say $250,000.

2. Market performance causes the paper value of your annuity to drop to $220,000.

3. You die.

4. Your heirs can collect the full amount of your initial investment -- $250,000 – less any withdrawals you have made.

It's easy to see why this death benefit would be an attractive on for investors. It ensures that the money you put into an annuity doesn't simply vanish into the ether. It provides both you and your dependents with some peace of mind that they can access the money you invested in the event of your death.

Some annuities now offer an option called a "stepped-up death benefit." This varies from the traditional death benefit because it makes market adjustments to the cash-out value of your annuity in the event that the paper value is higher than the actual value when you die.

In other words, the value may be adjusted upward every one to five years (provided that the value has increased) so that your heirs can collect the returns on your investment.

The primary issue I have with the death benefit is that it does nothing to help my clients while they are alive. The typical fee associated with this benefit is between 1.25% and 1.5% per year, every year that the annuity is in place. To put that into perspective, let's imagine that you invested $100,000 initially:

- In the first year, the death benefit would cost you $1,500 (assuming a rate of 1.5%)

- Over ten years, the death benefit would cost you $15,000

- Over twenty years, the death benefit would cost you $30,000

While you might have all the best intentions in terms of allowing your heirs to collect the money you invested, the truth is that the death benefit decreases the value of your account every year.[16]

The point of an annuity is to spend the money during your lifetime, not to pass it on to your heirs. A better option in terms of providing income for anybody who survives you is to buy a term life policy. The premiums are likely to be significantly less than the fees you would pay to buy the death benefit rider and the amount your beneficiaries get will not be impacted by the money you have withdrawn from your annuity.

Tax Deferral
Now let's talk about the tax deferral option.[17] The selling point for this option is always the same: when you buy the account, you can do so with pre-tax dollars and thus save

money in the long run. Proponents say that you can earn a return on your money without having to pay Uncle Sam.

Like so many things, this argument is true up to a point. Anybody can present you with a hypothetical situation to demonstrate the benefits of tax deferral, but you need to consider reality before making the decision to invest in this way.

One of the issues that I see with the way this option is presented is that very few of the online examples actually compare apples to apples. For example, they might give you an example of an initial investment of $10,000 that earns a 9% return per year on pre-tax dollars. Here, I'm going to use nice round numbers to show you what I mean.

Their numbers might show that if you had to pay taxes on your investment at an approximate rate of 33%, after 10 years your taxed investment might be worth, say $60,000, while the tax-deferred option would be worth $150,000. There's no question that $150,000 is a lot higher than $60,000 – but remember, that $60,000 is yours, clear and free. It has already been taxed and cannot be taxed again.

By contrast, the $150,000 is subject to tax. And even if you calculated the taxes using the same rate, 33%, the results can be misleading. That would put the post-tax value at about $100,000, but it's not really that simple.

One of the issues at hand, particularly when comparing a variable annuity with a mutual fund, is that the two investments are taxed at different rates. The money you withdraw from an annuity is taxed at the regular income rate – usually between 28% and 35%.

By contrast, the returns you earn on a mutual fund are considered capital gains and are typically taxed at a much lower rate.

What these examples show is that you absolutely need to work with an experienced financial advisor to help you work out the reality of what taxes you would pay if you choose a tax-deferred option.

I realize that it can be difficult for people who aren't well-versed in finance to wrap their heads around this issue. However, it's important to remember that you don't have to make these decisions alone. With the help of an advisor, you can take a look at your personal circumstances and make the best possible decisions for your financial future.

Annuitization

Another option to consider is how and if you should annuitize your investment. As a rule, there are three possible ways to annuitize.[18]

1. You can receive payments for the duration of your life.

2. You can receive payments for the duration of your life and your spouse's life.

3. You can receive annual payments for a fixed period.

You also, with a variable annuity, have the option of choosing between fixed payments and variable payments, which fluctuate based on the performance of your investments.

One of the big drawbacks of annuitization is that it limits you. If you decide that you want to defer the payments until later, you can't. If you decide that you need more of your money now, you can't do that either. You're locked in to whichever annuitization option you choose.

You might be wondering what not annuitizing does to the prospect of having guaranteed income. That's a good question to ask because it actually gets to the heart of why I recommend against it.

If you annuitize, as I said, you are locked into a particular payment schedule. Typically, annuitization benefits pay less if you predecease your spouse (or if they predecease you and own the account.)

If you don't annuitize, you have two options.[19]

1. You can instruct the institution that holds your account to send you monthly payments or quarterly payments, which you can stop or change at any time.

2. You can leave the money in your account and withdraw it as needed (within certain limitations).

The benefit of these two options is that you can have all the flexibility you need in terms of what to do with your money. You're not locked into any one option.

Guaranteed Income

The final benefit I want to talk about is guaranteed income. You might be tempted to think that this particular feature is one that you can take for granted regardless of the type of annuity you buy – but you would be wrong.

When a broker tries to sell an annuity to a client, he will usually present the annuity as though the income is guaranteed. He might tell you, for example, that you will get an annual protected return of between 6% and 7%, a guaranteed income stream of 5% per year after that.[20] But is that really true?

Let's look at what most people think happens with income guarantees to get an idea of the problem.

1. The principal and income guarantee part of an annuity says that you will be able to withdraw approximately 7% of your principal every year for a fixed period. Let's use 14 years as an example.

2. It likewise states that your protected balance will increase by approximately 6% per year in that time period – a figure that would guarantee you a 5% return every year for the rest of your life.

3. Most people believe that if they leave their money in place for 10 years and then withdraw it, they will have earned at least 5% to 7% per year that they can withdraw.

If it were that easy to make money from a variable annuity, I would never recommend anything else to my clients. I would be foolish – and possibly even derelict in my duties – if I didn't use all of my powers of persuasion to push variable annuities.

However – and as I suspect you have guessed – it is not that easy. The truth is that a variable annuity has an <u>actual value</u> based on the money you put into it, and a <u>income value</u> that's based on the money that it earns based on the underlying investments.

When the time comes to calculate what you can withdraw from the annuity, the valuation of the annuity inevitably comes from the actual value and not the income value. The same is true if you withdraw only the 5% of guaranteed income per year. Each withdrawal lowers both the actual value of your annuity and the income value.

In the event that you die, your heirs can only close out the annuity and collect what's left of its value minus any withdrawals you have made. In other words, people who buy this type of annuity almost never end up making a profit on their initial investment.

Here are the problems with the income guarantee as I see them – and this is what I always try to drive home to my clients.[21]

1. It's not really a guaranteed benefit. If it were, you would be able to cash in your balance after, say, 10 years, and walk away with, AT MINIMUM, the income value of your account. However, you can't do that. The only way you can enjoy this particular benefit is if you stay committed to the investment for the rest of your life.

2. It's also important to note that your guaranteed return stops as soon as you begin to make withdrawals from your account. So, for example, imagine that you were 10 years from retirement and you opened a annuity. The annuity would earn a return based on your investments. Once you begin to draw the balance down, it is no longer making a guaranteed return.

3. For the first 10 or 20 years you draw down on your annuity, all the insurance company is doing is paying you back your initial investment. There's no profit for you. If you made an initial investment of $100,000 that grew to $200,000 over 10 years, you might be able to withdraw $10,000 per year thereafter. For the 10 years, you would withdraw a grand total of $100,000 – which matches your initial investment exactly. Even after 20 years, you would only be taking the paper value of the account. In other words, the only way you will start to see a profit on your initial investment is if you live long enough to make annual withdrawals for more than 20 years.

4. The fourth consideration is that a variable annuity is susceptible to fluctuations in the market. You can't assume that you won't lose money on your initial investment, because you might. It depends on how

you allocate risk and what the market does during the period of your investment.

5. Finally, the guaranteed income stream for life rider is one of the more expensive features to add to an annuity. I'll talk more about the fees in the next chapter, but the bottom line is that your broker is likely to earn more of a profit if you buy this rider within a variable annuity.

It is important to note that many of these issues disappear if you choose a different type of annuity. However, the variable annuity that brokers love is fraught with risk for the buyer – that's you. I want to underline that you should think of your potential investment vehicles as being part of two different groups: Green Money and Red Money. Green Money being the safe investments and Red Money being those that are potentially at-risk.

Green - Safe Investments   **Red –At Risk Investments**

CD's
Checking
Savings
Treasuries
Fixed Annuities
Money Market

Stocks
Bonds
Mutual Funds
Variable Annuities
REITs

"I Know So" Money   **"I Hope So" Money**

Green Money is safe from risk and often time have guarantees built in – in fact many have lifetime benefits. The downside is they provide lower returns and less liquidity.

Red Money is at risk and you could potentially lose money in these investments due to market downturns. They do offer more growth and more liquidity.

In a retirement plan Green Money provides the core of your retirement fund while Red Money exists to allow growth. But there's a third option that can give you the safety and guarantees of Green Money – while providing the Growth and Liquidity options of Red Money.

Fixed Index Annuities give you many of these options and function in many ways as a hybrid investment vehicle. They allow you to invest safely, while obtaining much of the growth available from the market.

In the next chapter, I want to take a deep dive into the fee structures of annuities. The truth is that many annuities – particularly variable annuities – are characterized by hidden fees. The people who sell them often downplay the fees to make the annuities seem more attractive, and it's up to you to understand them and make sure that you know what you're buying – and what you're agreeing to pay – before you sign on the dotted line.

Chapter 4
Understanding Annuity Fee Structures

One of the areas that causes the most confusion and misunderstanding when it comes to annuities is the fee structure. Just as was the case with the features and language used to describe them, the intention is to try to minimize any objection you might have to the fees and make them sound as small (and inconsequential) as possible.

It can be difficult for the layperson to figure out what their fees will be in a real world situation. That's especially true of people who do not have a background in finance or accounting because the calculations can be complex.

It is for that reason that I decided to dedicate an entire chapter to explaining some of the most common fee structures used in annuities. You shouldn't make any decision about your retirement without having a thorough grasp of what the features and benefits of the annuity you choose will cost you.

To make sure that you understand each of the potential fee structures, I will break this down into three separate sections. The first will address the fee structures of fixed income annuities. The second will deal with the fee structures of fixed index annuities. And the third and final section of the chapter will address the fee structures of variable annuities.

What you will note as you read is that in some cases, the fees that are attached to these annuities are out in the open – and in other cases, they are masked or even hidden from view.

The decision you make regarding an annuity should take all fees into consideration to ensure that you know what you can expect in terms of fees and income.

Types of Annuity Fees

Let's start by reviewing the major types of fees that may be charged on an annuity account.[22] Some of these fees will not apply to certain types of annuities, so consider this an overview. Later in the chapter, I'll tell you where you can expect to see each fee.

Commission

One of the trickiest fees to see – because it's built into your annuity contract and thus is in many ways invisible – is the commission you pay to the company that provides the annuity.

It is fairly common for brokers and salespeople to claim that their annuities (particularly fixed income annuities) are fee-free because if you put $100,000 into an annuity, your balance will be $100,000. The commission isn't technically deducted from the principal, but it is still an expense associated with the account and it is very important for you to think of it that way when assessing the cost of your annuity.

Insurance Charges

Insurance charges are very common. They are also known as mortality and expense fees, or M & E fees - which only apply to variable annuities. Since insurance guarantees are typically included in the annuity automatically, these fees are to be expected.

In addition to covering M & E expenses, insurance charges also cover any administrative or selling expenses related to the contract.

Surrender Charges

Surrender charges are related to the amount of withdrawals an annuity account holder can take in the early years of the contract. They also place a surrender charge on all withdrawals that exceed the preset limit on withdrawals.

Surrender charges are one area where annuity account holders can get surprised by fees – not because they don't know about them, but because the charges can be quite significant and may be applicable for years.

For that reason, it is extremely important to be sure that you understand the surrender charges on your account and ask questions to clarify anything you do not understand.

Surrender Penalty Schedule For A Variable Annuity

YEAR	1	2	3	4	5	6	7	8	9	10	11+
	9%	9%	8%	8%	7%	6%	5%	4%	3%	2%	0%

Investment Management Fees

Investment management fees typically apply only to variable annuities. If you are familiar with the management fees on mutual funds, these fees are very similar.

The particular investment management fees charged are determined by the investment options on the annuity you choose, so they can vary greatly from company to company.

The best way to be clear about what fees are being assessed is to check your annuity prospectus and look for underlying funds to determine what the investment management fees are and how much you can expect to pay.

Rider Charges

The final type of fee that you need to be aware of is a rider charge. As their name suggests, rider charges are fees that accrue when you add certain optional guarantees (sometimes referred to as riders) to your annuity.

As you might expect, the expenses associated with these fees can add up quickly. For that reason, it is essential to thoroughly understand your annuity by reading its prospectus, asking questions, and reviewing the options with your financial advisor to ensure that you understand what you will be paying in fees.

Now that you understand some of the types of fees that you may be paying, let's take a closer look at the fee structures of the three major types of annuities.

Fee Structures of Fixed Income Annuities

A fixed income annuity should come with a statement of understanding that clearly explains all disclosed fees.[23] These should include only administrative fees and surrender charges, but remember, you should ask about commissions, too – some salespeople may not disclose these as fees.

The surrender period for a fixed annuity is typically between two and ten years, but it's important to check, especially if you think you may need to withdraw your money before the surrender period expires.

Fixed income annuities are generally the lowest cost type of annuity. They are also the most straightforward. Of course, you may choose to add riders that can increase your fees, so the key here is to be well-informed and absolutely certain that you understand the fees before you sign on the dotted line.

One thing to be careful of - if you decide to choose this type of annuity - is that you may end up losing it if you lock yourself into a fixed annuity for too long. For example, if there is a favorable change in interest rates, you may not be able to take advantage of it if you have, say, a 10-year surrender fee.

Fee Structures of Fixed Index Annuities

Now let's talk about the fee structures of fixed index annuities.[24] Remember, these are annuities whose returns are tied to a stock market index such as the Standard & Poor 500. There is typically a cap on how much you can make, but there is also a guarantee that you will never lose any of your principal due to stock market losses.

Many people working - or in retirement - like the idea of putting a portion of their money in a Fixed Index Annuity because they can't lose money.

The overall costs of most fixed index annuities is usually between 0.5% and 1.5% annually, so you'll have to be sure to keep that in mind before you buy one. Overall, that is a reasonably low cost.

Likewise, you should make sure to take any rider fees into consideration before making a decision. The bare bones fees are likely to be fairly low and thus attractive, but any additional benefits you add will increase your fees and your costs.

It may help to remember that fixed index annuities were not designed to compete with the stock market. Instead, they were designed to compete with CDs and other low-risk investments. These annuities have a higher potential than a regular fixed income annuity. Both have no have risk at all, unlike the risk inside a variable annuity.

Fixed index annuities are sometimes called hybrid annuities because they combine the investment flexibility of a variable annuity without the risk of losing money on the stock market.

Fee Structures of Variable Annuities

Finally, let's talk about the fee structures of variable annuities. As you know from the previous chapter, variable annuities offer the highest potential earnings of the three major types of annuities, but they also carry the highest risk of the three.

We previously discussed the most common riders that are added to variable annuities, including death benefits and investment management fees. These fees can add up.

The average overall cost of owning a variable annuity is about 3% per year including rider fees.[26] They also tend to pay fairly high built-in commissions, and it is essential that you find out what the commission is and how it will affect your overall costs.

It is possible to find some variable annuities that do not have surrender charges, which might be an attractive option for some people. However, the overall cost of these annuities – and the risks associated with them – may make the price too high to be comfortable for some investors.

Verifying Fees

When you make fee comparisons and get closer to making a decision about which annuity to buy, I highly recommend that you go directly to the carrier with questions about the fees. The reason is that you need to protect yourself.

A broker may have ulterior motives for pushing a particular annuity option. For example, he might hope that you will buy a variable annuity because his commissions will be higher than they would be with, say, a fixed index annuity.

By contrast, a customer service representative who works for the carrier does not have a stake in what you buy. Their only job is to provide you with accurate and timely answers to your questions. It's always best to get your answers directly from the carrier. That way you can be sure that nothing is getting lost in translation.

Looking beyond Fees
While evaluating the fees of any annuity you are considering is essential, you should also keep in mind that the bottom line is not the only consideration that might impact your decision.

Does an Annuity Suit Your Needs?
The first and most obvious thing to ask is if an annuity suits your purposes – and more specifically, if the particular type of annuity you are considering makes sense in light of your current financial situation and retirement goals for the future.

This is particularly important if somebody is trying very hard to sell you on a particular annuity option. We'll talk more later about why brokers are fond of variable annuities, but you should always consider the motivations and goals of the person who is selling to you and ask if they align with your personal goals.

How Strong is the Carrier?

Another key consideration is the strength of the carrier that issues your annuity contract. [27]

A lot of people stop evaluating when they get to the point where they understand the fees and riders that come with their annuity, but here's what you need to remember:

An annuity is only as strong as its carrier.

If you think back to the fall of 2008, you may remember that several large insurance carriers and brokers failed – or nearly failed – as a result of poor investment decisions.

One big carrier that comes to mind is AIG. The company survived that economic downturn only because the federal government bailed it out and provided the company with the money it needed to recover.

You can get a good idea of your carrier's financial strength by checking their rating with one of the four big rating companies:

- A.M. Best Company, Inc.
- Fitch Ratings
- Moody's Investor Services
- Standard & Poor's Insurance Rating Services

Many insurance carriers list their ratings on their marketing materials, but you should always check with the ratings companies directly.[28] Here's why:

1. Some insurance carriers may cherry-pick their highest ratings and not list others that cast the company in a more negative light.

2. The ratings are not consistent from company to company.

To get an idea of just how confusing and inconsistent the ratings can be from company to company, let's look at just one rating: A+.

To anybody who has attended school, an A+ probably sounds like an excellent rating. You might even expect – and not surprisingly – that it is the top rating available. You'd be wrong! Here's how the ratings shake out:

- For Moody's, an A+ is the company's second-highest of 14 total ratings categories.

- For both Fitch and Standard & Poor's, an A+ is their fifth highest rating – and even that is open to interpretation, because Fitch has a total of 24 ratings categories while Standard & Poor's has only 19.

- A.M. Best doesn't even have an A+ rating – they use a different scale entirely.

You should look beyond the ratings, too. For example, these companies also group companies into two mega-categories: secure and vulnerable. For the best possible result, you should choose a secure company with a rating that is at or near the top of the ratings categories available.

I realize this is a lot to consider, and I'll talk more later about how working with a fiduciary can help you understand the ins and outs of buying an annuity.

What I recommend is going in with a clear idea of what you want. Here are some questions to ask:

- What are your financial goals?

- What do you need from an annuity?

- How much income will you need at retirement?

- Do you understand the total amount you will be paying, including hidden fees, rider fees, and commissions?

- Are you confident that the insurance carrier backing your annuity is strong, financially secure, and likely to be around for the foreseeable future?

- Have you confirmed the fees and features directly with the carrier?

Answering these questions can help you make a decision, particularly when combined with the information in the next chapter.

That's where I'll talk about the pros and cons of buying an annuity, so keep reading to learn about what annuities can (and can't) do for you.

Chapter 5
Pros and Cons of Annuities

By now, I hope that you have a good understanding of the types of annuities, the features of annuities and what they really provide you, and the fee structures of the three most common types of annuities.

That's a good start, but now it's time to put what you have learned into perspective.

Like any investment or retirement strategy, there are pros and cons to investing some of your money in an annuity. You need to understand what those are to make an informed decision about what to do with the money you have saved for retirement.

In this chapter, I'll start with some of the pros of having an annuity. Some of the things I mention will expand on issues I have already raised in previous chapters, while others will be new to you. My goal is to be as thorough as possible because I want you to have all of the information you need.

After listing the pros of investing in an annuity, I'll cover the cons. Here again, my goal is to cover all potential cons with as much detail as possible so that you understand the risks and potential downsides of annuities. By the time you are done reading this chapter, you will have all of the information you need to make an honest and realistic evaluation of your financial situation and whether an annuity can help you plan for retirement.

The Pros of Annuities

As promised, let's start with the pros of buying an annuity. These are financial and personal advantages that may convince you to open an annuity account.

No Annual Contribution Limit

The first pro of choosing an annuity account as a way of preparing for retirement is that there are no limits on the annual contributions you can make to an annuity account.[29] However each company may limit the amount they are willing to take.

Why is this a benefit? Well, you may know that when you contribute to a 401K or an IRA, for example, there is a limit on the amount of money you can contribute each year. That may be fine for people who started saving for retirement early, but what do you do if you got a late start and you need to play catch up?

Opening an annuity is an excellent way to take some of your savings and put them in a safe place where you can collect them as needed later on.

If you are approaching retirement age and frustrated by the limitations on what you can do in terms of some other investment options, then an annuity may provide the solution you need to plan for retirement and be able to count on a guaranteed source of income after your retire.

No Required Withdrawals

Another key benefit of using a non-qualified annuity to prepare for your retirement is that you are not required to take money out on anybody's timetable except your own.

For example, people who own IRAs are obligated to begin taking money out when they reach the age of 70 ½, and they are penalized if they take money out before they reach the age of 59 ½.[30]

If you were concerned that you might outlive your spouse by a number of years and wanted some additional income that you could withdraw after their death, you could open a non-qualified annuity and leave it there until you needed it.

This is a very important benefit for people who might be unsure what their financial needs will be in the future. You have far more freedom in terms of when and how to take out money (assuming, of course, that you are in line with the carrier's surrender policy and fees.)

Lifetime Payments

Another key benefit of opening an annuity is that you can get a guaranteed payout – something that can help you plan for the future.[31]

One of the scariest things about retiring is that you may wonder how you will support yourself. What happens if something goes wrong with Social Security – or parts of it end up being privatized? What happens if you exhaust the money in your IRA?

By contract, if you choose a life payout option for your annuity account, you can be sure that you will have a fixed amount of money coming to you every year until you die – even if you have completely exhausted the money in your account.

That's why annuities are considered a form of insurance. They can provide a great deal of peace of mind and security – and that's the kind of thing that you can't get with an IRA or 401K.

Safe Investment

The thought of investing money – and having to worry about losing it – can be very frightening for people who are approaching their retirement years.
You may be eager to find ways to get your money to grow, but also fearful about taking too many chances with your nest egg.

Fixed income and fixed index annuities offer a nice middle ground. Fixed index annuities, in particular, allow you to invest your money – and potentially earn a return on it – without worrying that you'll end up losing everything.
As I have mentioned before, fixed index annuities have a cap on earnings but guarantee no loss in the market. They are aligned with a stock index such as the S & P 500, and that makes them a very stable and reliable investment.

It is worth noting here that this particular pro does not apply to variable annuities. Variable annuities, as I said earlier, are tied directly to the stocks you choose. If you choose unwisely or allocate too much of your portfolio to a losing stock, you could end up losing a significant amount of money.

Some investors are more risk-averse than others. I talk to a lot of people who are nervous about the prospect of investing in the stock market. It isn't uncommon for people who have lived long enough to see several big market downturns to be nervous about such things.

Fixed index annuities offer a safe and predictable way to earn a modest return on your investment. You're not going to get rich with a fixed index annuity, but you're not going to lose one penny of your money to the stock market.

Protection from Probate and Creditors

Investment accounts and portfolios can be difficult for your spouse and children to deal with if you predecease them.

One of the nicest benefits of opening an annuity account is that these accounts are exempt from probate in some areas. In other words, if you die, your annuity fund will not be used to pay off debts or otherwise satisfy the needs of probate should your estate require probate.[31]

That's a real plus for your heirs, who may be stressed and overwhelmed by the realities of dealing with your estate. And if you have a death benefit, they will have access to at least some of the money to help them going forward.

Likewise, in some states, annuity accounts may also be protected from creditors. This issue is related to probate but not identical to it. Later in life, it is not uncommon for people to accumulate medical debts that can eat into their retirement savings and income.

It is important to note here that the laws regarding creditors vary from state to state. You should plan to check with your state insurance commissioner, attorney and any other appropriate professional to verify what the laws are where you live.

Exemption from FAFSA Asset Status

One of the most common questions I get from my clients who have children is whether the money they put into an annuity will affect their kids' ability to qualify for federal financial aid to help them get through college.

This is, in my opinion, a huge pro in favor of annuities. When you open an annuity, the money you put into it does not count as an asset when you fill out your FAFSA application.[32]

In other words, if you want to set money aside for retirement by opening an annuity, you can do so without worrying that it will prevent your child from qualifying for need-based assistance for college tuition and related expenses.

I will have more to say on this topic in the cons section because there is another form where the money you put into an annuity must be reported. Keep that in mind – this is more of a mixed pro than an unqualified one. Again, please check with proper legal counsel as laws change.

Minimal Management Required
The final benefit I want to talk about has to do with the management and effort required to maintain an annuity.

The truth is there is very little, particularly if you have a fixed annuity of any kind. The money goes into your account according to the agreement you signed. Since a fixed index annuity is tied to a stock market index, you don't have to worry about shuffling investments. You can merely track the index itself as a way of keeping track of your investment.

In other words, this is an extremely low maintenance way to invest your money. But it is still important to consult your advisor as needed. Stock indices tend to be far more stable than any one individual stock, so it is unlikely you will experience the dramatic ups and downs that you would if you invested in the stock market directly.

If you like the hands-on approach you might see this as a disadvantage, but many of my clients find it a relief not to have to worry about their investment. They can sit back and relax knowing that their money is safe and will be ready for them when they need it.

The Cons of Annuities
Now that we have covered the pros, let's talk about the cons of opening an annuity account. These accounts have a lot going for them, but there are definitely some negatives to consider before you invest in one.

Lack of Liquidity
The first potential con you need to be aware of is that annuities do not give you the same flexibility as some other investment options when it comes to withdrawing money.[33]

Earlier, we talked about surrender fees and how they can eat into your investment if you don't adhere to the terms of your annuity contract.

If you invested in stocks, for example, you would have the right to sell those stocks and liquidate your assets at any time – and without paying a penalty. Of course, you would lose money if you sold at a price lower than your buy price, but you would be able to assess that in the moment and make a decision about what to sell.

With an annuity, you have no choice. The money is where it is and if you are still within the specified surrender period, you are likely to end up paying a hefty surrender fee to withdraw your money.

No Guarantors
When you deposit money with a bank, you know that your deposit is backed by the Federal Deposit Insurance Corp. (FDIC) However, there is no such guarantee with an annuity.[34]

Does that mean you have no protection? Of course not. Each state is required to have an insurance guarantee organization, and they provide annuity holders with some protection in the event of a failure.

Most states have minimum guarantee protection for fixed annuities but no guaranteed protection for variable annuities. Also many of the fixed annuities hold cash reserves to protect the investor unlike variable annuities.

However, the protection is not as thorough as it would be with the FDIC. That's why I urged you in the last chapter to take the time to check out the annuity company's financial ratings for yourself instead of counting on their marketing materials or reassurances of financial strength.

This is a con in that it is the opposite of a pro, but I want to emphasize that it is also one that can be largely offset by careful research and evaluation. It is unlikely that an insurance company with top of the line ratings from the major agencies is going to run into a problem big enough that you would lose your investment.

Annual Fees

Certain forms of annuities charge annual fees, and they can range between approximately 1% and 3%.[36] Keep in mind that if you open a $100,000 annuity, that works out to $1,000 to $3,000 a year.

To get an idea of how that might affect you, imagine that your annuity is earning an annual return of 6%. If your annual fee with a variable annuity is 3%, it is essentially cutting your earnings in half every year. Worse if the market is down 30% with a variable annuity and the fees 3%, you lose 33% for the year!

That can make a big difference when it comes to the paper value of your annuity, so make sure to keep it in mind when evaluating what to do with your money.

Some Annuities Won't Pay Heirs

As I mentioned earlier in the book, most individual annuities will only pay to the person whose name is on the annuity. That means that if you were to open an annuity and then die a few months after you did so, the money might stay with the insurance company.

However, this is rare and more common with older contracts. Most contracts today will provide the account balance to the named beneficiaries at the time of death.

Complicated Contracts

Another potential downside to keep in mind is that many annuities, particularly variable annuities, have incredibly complicated contracts that are difficult for a layperson to understand.

Variable annuities usually come with a large prospectus that explains all of the ins and outs of the annuity. It includes information about payouts, surrender periods, fees, and so on.

As you might expect, the language used in these contracts is not easy to understand. In my opinion, lawyers write them and in many cases, their job is to obfuscate rather than enlighten. They keep things deliberately vague, talk around issues instead of addressing them directly, and so on.

All in all, you should not consider buying any annuity if you cannot understand the prospectus. If you have questions, ask them. If you don't like the answers, ask again.

It's also a good idea to have your own lawyer or financial advisor review the contract and ask questions. The reason you hire a financial advisor is so that they can bring their expertise and experience to bear on your behalf.

Hidden Fees and Other Fees

You already know that many annuities – variable annuities in particular – have hidden fees built into them. I call them hidden because they do not appear on your statement. Instead, they are deducted first. Once they are, the number on your statement is meant to represent the value of your account.

In other words, if your investment in a variable annuity earned a 7% return in a given year, the fees would be taken out first and then you would see, say, a 3% return instead. That might seem like a respectable number – and it is, until you realize that the company ultimately collected more than you did.[37]

What are the fees that fall into the category of hidden fees? I would include:

- Mortality and expense risk charges (M & E)
- Administrative fees
- Subaccount Fees
- Rider Fees

All of these are deducted from what you see on your account statement. From the layperson's perspective, it might appear simply that the investments in the variable annuity did not perform as well as expected.

However, if you pay attention to the underlying fee structure, the truth is that the insurance company is taking its cut out of your profits and not disclosing how much they earned.

Does the contract you sign allow them to do that? Yes, it does. But there's no question that a lot of annuity holders are misled by the practice. They don't understand how many fees are included or how much they are paying.

Included in CSS Profile
Earlier, I told you that one of the benefits of annuities is that they do not need to be reported as an asset on the FAFSA financial aid form. That is a significant benefit for some families because it helps to maximize the aid you can get to send your children to college.

However, I also told you that I would revisit that issue because there was an exception. It's called the CSS Profile.[38]

The CSS Profile is a financial aid form that is used – in addition to FAFSA – by about 300 colleges and universities nationwide.

It is used to determine non-government aid eligibility. In other words, if your child might qualify for aid from the university itself, you would have to fill out the CSS Profile.

Not all annuities must be reported on the CSS Profile, only those that are deemed to be non-qualified. If the annuity you buy does qualify, you'll have to list those assets and you will be expected to use them to offset your child's college expenses.

Since we have already talked about surrender charges at length, it should be easy to see where this is going.
Factors to be considered:

- The cost of room and board at the college your child attends
- Your other assets
- The amount of money in your annuity

You might end up having to withdraw money from the annuity to pay for part of your child's education. In the event that your financial situation is such that you need to withdraw a substantial amount, you may also end up also having to pay a hefty surrender fee for the privilege of using your own money to send your child to school

This can - be in many cases - an avoidable situation. There are thousands of colleges in the United States and many of them do not use the CSS Profile. Also, not every annuity must be reported.

The key is to do some research before you buy and make sure you understand whether the annuity you choose needs to be reported on the CSS Profile.

Lack of Control
One of the biggest misconceptions about variable annuities is that they give the investor more control over their money than other types of annuities.

I think it's important to talk about why that is - because the perception is very far from the reality of the situation.

With a variable annuity, you have the right to choose how to invest your money. If there's a particular stock you like, you can choose to allocate part of your annuity funds to it, linking the annuity's overall performance to the performance of the stocks you choose.

That sounds good on the surface – and if you get very lucky with your investment choices - I suppose it could be a good choice. There's no limit on the amount of profit you can earn with a variable annuity, so if you made stellar investments you could end up better off than you would with, say, a fixed index annuity.

However, the other element of variable annuities is that you don't have the same freedom to withdraw your money that you would with other investments. Of course you can shift your money and sell stocks, but what do you do if the entire market is in a downturn?

The only way to get your money out of the market is to withdraw it from the annuity. And I'm sure you can guess where I'm going with this. If you withdraw early, you'll have to pay a hefty surrender fee

Brokers who sell annuities often try to use the idea that you can withdraw up to 10% of your account balance each year as a benefit. If you could be sure that none of the following things would happen, that might be true:

- The stock market flounders or crashes and you want to switch to a different, less risk investment

- Your financial needs change dramatically due to a healthcare crisis and you need money to pay for your medical bills

- You want to buy a smaller home and need money from the annuity as a down payment

- You have any other unexpected financial need or crisis that means that you need to get immediate access to your money

In other words, if the world were a completely predictable place and you never had to worry about being taken by surprise by anything, then investing in a variable annuity might be a good way to go.

However, you know as well as I do that the world is unpredictable and even chaotic at times.

Of course, surrender fees are an issue even with fixed income and fixed index annuities, but those investments are at least predictable – provided that you took the time to determine that the insurance company itself is financially strong and that there is no downside risk in the stock market.

These pros and cons illustrate why the decision to buy an annuity is a complex one. Some annuities have far more items on the pro list than on the con list – and some are the reverse, with more ticks in the con column than in the pro column.

My key goal in presenting these pros and cons is not to scare you away from buying an annuity. Rather, it is to make sure that you understand that there is a wide difference between a good annuity and a bad one.

As a financial advisor, I work closely with my clients to make sure they understand the features and fees of any annuity they are considering buying. I crunch the numbers and share them so that the clients know exactly what they are getting – and what they will be paying in fees.

On the whole, I think buying an annuity can be a very wise investment decision for some people, particularly those who want a safe and predictable investment and the reassurance of guaranteed income. However, certain annuities do not actually fulfill these requirements, and those are the ones that I want to make sure that my clients – and you – understand.

In the next chapter, I'm going to dig more deeply into a topic I have already mentioned several times. Brokers love variable annuities – and it's time to talk about why that is true.

Chapter 6
Why Brokers Like Variable Annuities

Earlier in the book, I told you that it is always a good idea – and a smart approach – to ask yourself what the person selling you an annuity gains if you buy it.

Nowhere is that more true than when a broker wants you to buy a variable annuity. The truth, as you might expect, is that a broker can benefit from selling you a variable annuity in a number of ways – and some of those ways are the opposite of beneficial for you.

Does that mean that every broker is out to line their pockets while simultaneously hurting you? Of course not.

What it does mean, though, is that you should proceed with caution when dealing with a broker. The old Latin saying is *Caveat Emptor*, which means Buyer, Beware.

It might feel cynical or harsh to enter into a transaction asking whether the person on the other end of it is honest or scrupulous, but here's what I ask you to remember as you read this chapter.

This is your money we're talking about. It's your retirement – and your future.

You have every right to be cautious and skeptical. In fact, it's the smart thing to do. The last thing you want to do is make a choice about what to do with a sizable chunk of your savings only to find out after the fact that you misunderstood the features or fees.

There's another old saying that says:

Marry in haste, repent at leisure.

I think that should be rewritten to say:

Invest in haste, repent at leisure.

In this chapter, I'll explain what you need to know when a broker is trying to convince you to buy a variable annuity. I'll also tell you how brokers benefit from the sale of variable annuities. *And finally, I'll share with you what some of the experts have to say about the risks associated with variable annuities, including the AARP and financial experts - such as Suze Orman, Dave Ramsey, and Jane Bryan Quin - advise against buying variable annuities.*

What to Know When a Broker Wants You to Buy a Variable Annuity

I have already mentioned several times that brokers tend to like variable annuities and recommend them to their clients. Now it's time to talk about why - so you understand what's going on in a broker's head when they try to sell you one.

The first thing you need to know is that a broker's bottom line is always his bottom line. Brokers only earn money when they get a commission. Most are not on any kind of a salary.

If you have ever worked a job that is based on commission, you know that it can feel unpredictable at best and downright scary at worst. There may be times when you literally don't know where your next paycheck will come from.

That's the reality that brokers deal with every day. They have to wheel and deal constantly to earn a living. Their minds are always thinking about their next commission.

Also the Broker can only offer whatever product the company he works for has to offer. But an Independent Advisor can offer you everything available on the market based on your best interests.

As a compassionate person, you can probably understand that. Living on commission is not comfortable for most people. When you rely on commission, it can be unnerving to have financial commitments like mortgages, insurance premiums, and tuition. What happens if the next sale doesn't come through – or the next one after that?

However, when you make an investment in your own future, you can't be thinking about compassion for the broker's plight. That's not going to help you make the best investment choices for yourself. You have to be focused on what a particular investment is going to do for you.

I have seen many people go down with the financial Titanic simply because they felt loyal to their broker!

Remember, the commissions on a variable annuity are hidden, meaning that they don't show up on your statement. They are usually built in to a contract, and that being the case, a lot of people don't think about them when they buy a variable annuity.

Perhaps the most important thing to remember as you listen to a broker pitch you on a variable annuity is that they have a motive for doing so. No broker sells ANY variable annuity out of the goodness of his or her heart. They sell because they earn big when they do, it's that simple.

In many cases, it is in their best interest to keep you in the dark about how much of your money they stand to take if they can talk you into a variable annuity.

Does this mean that there are no scrupulous brokers out there? Of course not. However, it is safe to say that even a scrupulous broker needs to earn a living. Again, they're not selling you on the idea of an annuity because they think it's great for _you_. They're doing it because it's great for _them_.

You need to take a step back, keep their likely motives in mind, and ask whether a variable annuity is right for you. Don't worry about what they tell you. Check everything out for yourself.

For example, the government agency that oversees variable annuities is the Financial Industry Regulatory Authority, also known as FINRA. You can check out any broker by using their search function at Finra.com.

If you make the decision to work with a broker to buy an annuity, then you must commit to being an informed consumer. Here's how to approach it:

1. Go into the transaction with a realistic idea of when you might need your money. How heavily will you be relying on the annuity? Do you have other sources of income? You need to have a clear picture of your financial situation before you make any investment decisions.

2. Allow the broker to make his pitch, and take notes. It's always a good idea to keep track of what you were told about the annuity you are considering.

3. Ask the broker point blank whether they will be earning a commission if you buy the annuity. If they say no, be VERY skeptical. Why else would they sell it to you? If they say yes, ask them how much. Don't let them get away with hemming and hawing. Demand a straight answer.

4. Don't agree to any rider or benefit that you don't think you will use. For example, if you are a single or widowed and have no children, you probably don't need to worry about a death benefit. You can't take your money with you and you'll be better off using the money during your lifetime.

5. Check out the broker using the FINRA link to make sure they are scrupulous.

6. Double check what the broker tells you about the variable annuity fees with the insurance carrier who will be holding the annuity.

If you follow all of these steps, you can at least be sure that you understand what you are buying. Too many people make hasty decisions about buying variable annuities, but it's important to be an informed consumer.

Warnings against Buying Variable Annuities

To close out the chapter, I want to share with you some of what other financial experts say about variable annuities. My goal is to make sure that you understand what they are and what you'll be paying, but you don't know me. Perhaps you need to hear it from more than one person to understand the truth about variable annuities.

For example, **Jane Bryant Quinn**, a nationally recognized financial expert who has written for the Wall Street Journal and other publications. Here's what she says about variable annuities:

"I cannot imagine a personal finance situation where I'd recommend a Variable Annuity as a good idea."

Another well-known financial guru is **Suze Orman** - who is known both for books and for her numerous television appearances. Whether you love her or hate her – here's what she has to say about Variable Annuities.

"Q: My financial advisor is recommending that I buy a variable annuity within my retirement account. What should I do?

A: Get yourself another financial advisor pronto!"

Dave Ramsey is another well-known financial expert who doesn't care for variable annuities.

"Dave isn't a fan of annuities, and there are plenty of reasons why. One of the main reasons is that annuities have significant expenses that reduce the growth of your investment. Annuities also have surrender charges on early withdrawals that can limit access to your money in the first few years after you buy the annuity."

Finally, let's talk about what **Jim Cramer** has to say about variable annuities.

"Jim also doesn't like the fact that some annuities restrict account holders' ability to make changes to their investments.[45] The insurance carrier's ultimate goal is always to work to protect their future earnings – just as a broker's goal is to maximize their commissions."

And it's not just individuals who are warning against variable annuities.
For example, **Baron's** - one of the most prestigious financial newspapers in the world had this to say:

"Over the past decade, assets held in variable annuity contracts have increased rapidly, to more than $900 billion - due to a combination of deceptively clever marketing and the sales efforts of agents motivated by high commissions."

Other important financial publications like the **Wall Street Journal** also warn against variable annuities.

"Sellers, Brokers do well on fees, but some buyers turn sour when they read the fine print."

The highly influential **Fortune Magazine** had even stronger words when it comes to variable annuities.

"Variable Annuities are being touted as new and improved. But they still cost too much. Tax-deferred variable annuities could be called the cockroaches of the investment world."

Even the **AARP** has weighed in on variable annuities.

"Variable Annuity customers pay a variety of annually recurring expenses, including mortality expenses, distribution fees, administration fees, investment fees and fees for optional extra features. The total of these fees range from 2.4% a year to more than 4%."

What I hope you will take away from all of this is that buying a variable annuity is something you should only do with extreme caution. Variable Annuities pay commissions two to twenty times higher than Mutual Funds. Variable annuities are sold more aggressively than fake Gucci handbags on the street of New York City. A variable annuity is not a first remedy for retirement planning. It is one option among many.

The most important thing you can do if you want to consider a variable annuity is to make sure that you understand everything before you move forward with a purchase. Remember, these accounts are complicated by design. They may work for some investors, but they are certainly less than ideal for others.

The best way to protect yourself is to ask questions, and to work with a financial advisor who has experience with variable annuities. These annuities can be difficult to understand even for people who have spent a lifetime working with investors. You should be aware of that fact and act accordingly. Don't assume that you can figure it all out as a layperson.

In the next and final chapter, I will share some information about the importance of working with a fiduciary standard financial advisor. Just as you should not make hasty decisions about investing in an annuity, you should not jump into a financial advisory relationship without doing your homework.

Chapter 7
Why You Should Only Work with a Fiduciary Financial Advisor

Who do you trust when it comes to helping you make financial decisions that will impact your future and your retirement?

That is a question that too few people ask, in my opinion. They are hungry for advice and they want to make good decisions, but they lack the information they need to make an informed decision about who gives them financial advice.

The sad truth is that it is very easy for unscrupulous people to make a living advising uninformed investors about how to use their money. You have probably heard more than one story about some innocent person who lost their life savings because they trusted someone who turned out to be a crook.

Indeed, we need look no further than Bernie Madoff to understand how easy it is for dishonesty to cost honest people everything they have. Madoff might be an extreme example, but he's also a useful one because his story illustrates the dangers of making hasty decisions about trusting people with your money.

My opinion is that trusting a broker or anybody who doesn't adhere to the highest possible standards with your money is a mistake. In this chapter, I'll explain the difference between a fiduciary standard and a non-fiduciary financial advisor. I'll also explain why the best advocate for your retirement is a fiduciary standard.

The Difference between a Fiduciary Standard and a Non-Fiduciary Financial Advisor

I want to start by talking about the differences between a fiduciary standard and a non-fiduciary financial advisor.[46] This is a topic that not many people understand - but it can have a significant impact on your investments and your ability to retire.

Here are the primary differences that you need to know about:

1. A fiduciary standard is overseen by the Securities and Exchange Commission (SEC) and is seen to be in a position of trust. Their job is to act in your best interest without regard for their own earnings or concerns. They have access to your accounts and other financial information. By contrast, a non-fiduciary standard is not bound by the same high standards. While there is a requirement that fee-based advisors must not act against the direct interests of a client, they are still primarily motivated by the fees they earn.

2. The Good Faith and Best Interest standards that apply to fiduciaries are strict and specifically designed to protect the client – that's you. A fiduciary must, at all times, put the best interests of their clients before their own. That's what it means to have a fiduciary

responsibility to someone. There are no divided loyalties, whereas the same cannot be said of non-fiduciary, fee-based advisors.

3. The standards that non-fiduciaries must adhere to is known as the Suitability Standard. Simply, it states that a non-fiduciary must steer clients toward investment options that are suitable for their financial needs and goals. It also states that fees must be kept to a reasonable level, and that non-fiduciaries must not manipulate their clients' accounts to generate more fees, a process known as churning.

4. The fiduciary standards state, in no uncertain terms, that a fiduciary must immediately disclose any conflict of interest that might bring the fiduciary's interests and concerns into conflict with the client's, even if there is no immediate conflict present. This provision is in place to protect investors and ensure that fiduciaries always keep their clients' best interests front and center. Fiduciaries are also specifically prohibited from pursuing any financial investment or opportunity where there is even the potential of a conflict of interest.

5. By contrast, non-fiduciaries are bound by a significantly lower standards. They are still required to disclose conflicts of interest, but they are held to what is known as a "best execution" standard. It says that they must complete any transaction as efficiently as possible and as inexpensively as possible.

6. Fiduciaries must operate under a requirement of complete transparency when it comes to their fees and charges. There can be no hidden fees or confusion

when dealing with a fiduciary. They are legally obligated to disclose everything to you and may be penalized if they do not. Here again, the standard is lower for non-fiduciaries. They are supposed to disclose fees but it's a less stringent requirement. You do run the risk of getting hit with unexpected or undisclosed fees if you deal with a non-fiduciary advisor.

7. Fiduciaries must answer to the SEC, which describes their fiduciary responsibilities to their clients and specifies the standards to which they must adhere. They may also have to answer to certain state regulatory agencies depending on where they do business. Non-fiduciary standards are regulated by FINRA. In other words, both types of advisors have professional standards to adhere to, but they are administered by separate agencies.

What I hope you can see from this is that while non-fiduciary advisors do have standards that regulate what they do, the standards are far stricter for fiduciaries.

A fiduciary must adhere to the highest possible professional standards and is legally bound to act in the best interests of his clients. Non-fiduciaries are held to a far lower standard, and that means that people who work with them may be at an increased risk.

Broker	Independent Fiduciary
Can Sell only employer-approved Products	Ability to Access All Products and Services
Paid to Sell	Legally Bound To Provide Best Advice
Paying Commissions for Selling Funds	Paying Flat Fee For Advice
Suitability Standard (Worst for Customers)	Fiduciary Standard (Best or Customers)
Constrained by Employer	Independent
Nondeductible Commissions	Advisory Fees (May Be Deductible)
Large Office Beholden To a Large Corporation Only Has Access to Corporation's Products	1-4 Team Office Has Large Back Office Support Has Access to the Best Options

Why a Fiduciary Standard is the Best Advocate for Your Retirement

Now let's talk about why a fiduciary standard is the best possible advocate for your retirement.

In order to become a fiduciary standard, financial advisors must undergo rigorous training to earn a spot on the Fiduciary Registry. They must learn the relevant regulations and demonstrate that they understand them to earn the designation.[47]

The question to ask yourself when choosing a financial advisor is who you would rather have making financial recommendations to you?

1. *Someone who is legally bound to put their own interests aside and provide you with complete, unbiased, and independent analysis of investments as they relate to your particular needs and financial situation?*

2. *Someone who is bound to a lower standard and may be motivated to convince you that certain investments are worthwhile based on their own financial needs and goals?*

If you're like most people, you quickly chose the first option as the better of the two. You want a financial advisor who is honor-bound (and legally required) to act as your financial advocate in all situations.

Think about it this way. Planning for retirement is critical. If you don't do it properly, you may end up having far less money than you need to pay for your living expenses. You may not be able to have the retirement you want to have.

Financial planning is a complicated thing to do. Even an investor with a relatively simple portfolio can become confused when dealing with the ins and outs of their investments. When you are not an expert, it is all too easy to miss essential pieces of information or nuances of a contract.

When that happens, you may end up being surprised by hidden fees or confusing clauses that limit your access to money or penalize you for early withdrawal. When you work with a fiduciary standard, you can be sure that the person who is making investment recommendations is taking the time to:

- Look closely at both your current financial situation and your retirement needs so that all decisions and recommendations are made with your best interest in mind.

- Examine all contracts, including annuities, and taking the time to understand every nuance of them, including disclosed and hidden fees, surrender periods, commissions, and any other factors that might impact your retirement.

- Disclose any and all fees they are charging to you immediately and with total transparency so that you always understand how much you are paying for their services.
- Disclose any potential conflict of interest to you so that you can make an informed decision in the event that such a conflict exists.

In other words, working with a fiduciary standard is akin to working with a loyal friend – someone who has your best financial interest in mind at all times and is legally and morally bound to act in those interests even when they might be in conflict with their own best interest.

That is a powerful thing and it's why I recommend that everybody work with a fiduciary standard to plan their retirement. Retirement is not something you should trust to someone who adheres to a lower standard. This is your life, and this is your money. <u>You deserve the best.</u>

The bottom line is that you can find a fiduciary standard financial advisor, and in my opinion, you should. Why would you voluntarily work with someone who has no obligation to be transparent with fees, disclose conflicts of interest, and make recommendations that serve your financial needs and plans? Why would you do that when there are alternatives available?

Therefore, my strong recommendation is that the only type of financial advisor you should work with when planning your retirement is a fiduciary standard. Regardless of the type of financial advisor you work with, you will be paying a fee. Since you are going to be paying someone to give you financial advice and help you plan for retirement, it makes sense to choose a person who holds themselves to the highest possible professional and ethical standards.

It is important to note that the fees you pay to a fiduciary are typically based on your assets, while non-fiduciary brokers only earn commission. Working with a fiduciary puts you in the best possible financial position in terms of security.

As you can see, there is a big difference between working with a fiduciary and working with a non-fiduciary. That doesn't mean that all non-fiduciaries are unworthy of your trust, but for many investors, the presence of the fiduciary standard provides a level of comfort and security that is simply not available in the absence of a fiduciary standard. You deserve the very best when it comes to your retirement, and working with a fiduciary standard means that you can be sure to get it. You have worked very hard for your money and you deserve to be able to enjoy it.

Summary

Thank you for reading *The Truth About Annuities*. I hope that you have found the information in this book to be both helpful and enlightening.

The number one thing I hope you will take away from this book is that planning for retirement is not something to postpone. You may or may not decide to invest in an annuity of some kind, but you should absolutely start planning now if you have not already done so.

The problem with delaying is that you might easily reach a point where catching up enough to ensure that you have what you need is impossible. Most people, in my experience, vastly underestimate the amount of money they will need to retire.

Begin by having a discussion with the advisor who gave you this book. If he gave it to you, it's because he felt it was important to consider your financial future now rather than later.

I do think that investing in an annuity can be a good way to protect some of your money and have the reassurance and security of predictable and guaranteed outcome for the rest of your life.

The key things you should be considering when evaluating annuities are:

- The overall structure of the annuity – is it a fixed income annuity, a fixed index annuity, or a variable annuity?

- How long is the surrender period and what are the surrender charges? This is key because it can have a significant impact on your ability to access your money in the future.

- What riders do you actually need to suit your particular financial circumstances and retirement plans? Remember, brokers will try to sell you on as many riders and options as possible.

- What are the fees associated with the annuity? Make sure to inquire about hidden fees. Many annuities, as I previously stated, include built-in fees that will not show up on your account statement. You owe it to yourself to be fully informed about what it is truly costing you to own an annuity.

Caution is especially required when evaluating any form of variable annuity. Variable annuities are complicated by design. They often come with a prospectus that can be hundreds of pages long.

The reason these documents are so lengthy is that the companies who issue them – and the brokers who sell them – are counting on you not reading them. They want to keep their fees hidden and the penalties obscure.

While you should work with a financial advisor, you should also be aware that it is your responsibility – to both yourself and your family – to act as your own best financial advocate. That means that you need to be skeptical, ask as many questions as needed, and get professional help and advice to make sure that you haven't missed anything.

Case Studies

Here are three very common scenarios I see every week regarding people with Variable Annuities.

- I didn't know I even had a Variable Annuity
- I had no idea the fees were that outrageous
- I was told I didn't have any fees
- I think the fees are less than 1% per year
- I was told there are no fees
- If the market loses 40% I can't lose any of my principle
- My money is protected from any downside market loses
- I didn't think I could lose any money in the stock market
- I thought my principle was protected
- My heirs always get the full death benefit even if account goes to zero from withdrawals
- I was told there was no charge to have the death benefit feature
- I was told me and my spouse are guaranteed a payout for both our lives

- I was advised that I get a joint payout option to protect my spouse

Don't Feel Bad…It's not your fault!

Here are how some Variable Annuities compared to Fixed Index Annuities…

Example 1

Features	Variable Annuity	Fixed Income Annuity
Cost	3.5% +/-	1% +/-
Approx Fees p/y	$9,100	$2,600
Low Fees'	No	Yes
Market Protection	No	Yes
Layered Protection	No	Yes
Death Benefit Charge	Yes	No
Critical Illness	Limited	Yes
Terminal Illness	Limited	Yes
Health Care Doubler	Limited	Yes

Will pay over $225,000 over the next 25 years in fees if account value stays the same.

With $9,100 in fees for the past 5 years **$45,500 in fees** have been paid on the Variable Annuity and **it has only earned $35,000.**

Current Annuity Value: **$259,692**
Value After Surrender Charges: **$245,500**

Value With New Fixed Income Annuity:
10% Bonus x $245,500 = **$270,000**

Example 2

Features	Variable Annuity	Fixed Income Annuity
Cost	3% +/-	1% +/-
Approx Fees p/y	$10,500	$3,500
Low Fees'	No	Yes
Market Protection	No	Yes
Layered Protection	No	Yes
Death Benefit Charge	Yes	No
Critical Illness	Limited	Yes
Terminal Illness	Limited	Yes
Health Care Doubler	Limited	Yes
Guaranteed Income:		
Primary Income	$2,821 (Single)	$3,100 (Joint)
Spouse's Income	$4,179 (Single)	$4,601 (Joint)
Joint Income	$11,743 (Joint)	$12,461 (Joint)

Annuity Replacement Form

Existing Annuity	Proposed Annuity
Issue Date:_____	Transfer $_____ Bonus $_____
Company:_____	Company:_____
Contract Name:_____	Contract Name:_____
M & E Fees:_____	M & E Fees:_____
Admin Fees:_____	Admin Fees:_____
Total Fees: _____	Total Fees: _____
Owners: _____	Owners: _____
Annuitant: _____	Annuitant: _____
Beneficiary: _____	Beneficiary: _____
Original Deposit Value: _____	Original Deposit Value: _____
Date: _____ Basis: _____	Date: _____ Basis: _____
Current Value:_____	Current Value:_____
Surrender Value:_____	Surrender Value:_____
Death Benefit:_____	Death Benefit:_____
LB Cost: ___%	LB Cost: _____%
Compounded @____ to age _____	Compounded @_____ to age ___
Annuitization Schedule:_____	Annuitization Schedule:_____
Withdrawal Benefit:_____%	Withdrawal Benefit:_____%
Free Withdrawal:_____%	Free Withdrawal:_____%
# Money Managers: _____	# Money Managers: _____
Sub Accounts:_____	Sub Accounts:_____
Performance:_____	Performance:_____
Fixed Account:_____%	Fixed Account:_____%
MVA:_____	MVA:_____

If you do decide to buy an annuity, Fixed Index Annuities are the ones that I most frequently recommend to my clients. I like these annuities because they offer similar tax benefits to other retirement accounts, they offer the opportunity for a higher return on your investment than a fixed income annuity, and they are significantly less risky than variable annuities.

Buying an annuity can help you prepare for the future by providing you with a reliable and predictable source of income to supplement your other retirement income, including Social Security and pension plans. It probably doesn't make sense to have an annuity be your only source of retirement income outside of Social Security, but buying one can be a good way to obtain some financial security in your golden years.

Finally, I just want to remind you again that if you decide to work with a financial advisor – **and I strongly recommend that you do – the best choice is to work with a fiduciary standard.**

Fiduciary standards are held to the highest possible professional and ethical standards. They are bound to provide the best advice to their clients, always keeping the client's best financial interest in mind.

They must be completely transparent when disclosing their fees, and they must also disclose, immediately, any real or potential conflict of interest. These standards ensure that you will not have to worry about being taken advantage of by someone unscrupulous. You – and your retirement money – will be protected.

Your retirement years should be the best years of your life. You have worked hard to earn what you have and now is the time to enjoy it. It is natural to want to have a safe and happy retirement – and to be confident that the financial steps you have taken will protect you, your spouse, and your heirs.

Thank you again for reading. If you would like to get more information about me or my practice, please visit TonyHansmann.com.

I look forward to hearing from you.

Sources

The Truth about Annuities – Citations

1. Retirement Savings Survey. (n.d.). Retrieved June, 2017, from http://time.com/money/4258451/retirement-savings-survey/
2. Fixed Annuity. (n.d.). Retrieved June, 2017, from http://www.investopedia.com/terms/f/fixedannuity.asp
3. Variable Annuity. (n.d.). Retrieved June, 2017, from http://www.investopedia.com/terms/v/variableannuity.asp
4. Getting the Whole Story on Variable Annuities. (n.d.). Retrieved June, 2017, from http://www.investopedia.com/articles/04/111704.asp
5. All About Deferred Annuities. (n.d.). Retrieved June, 2017, from https://www.thebalance.com/all-about-deferred-annuities-2389020
6. What are Surrender Charges? (n.d.). Retrieved June, 2017, from https://www.thebalance.com/what-are-surrender-charges-2389029
7. Immediate Payment Annuity. (n.d.). Retrieved June, 2017, from http://www.investopedia.com/terms/i/immediatepaymentannuity.asp
8. Getting the Whole Story on Variable Annuities. (n.d.). Retrieved June, 2017, from http://www.investopedia.com/articles/04/111704.asp

9. All About Deferred Annuities. (n.d.). Retrieved June, 2017, from https://www.thebalance.com/all-about-deferred-annuities-2389020

10. Ultimate Guide to Retirement. (n.d.). Retrieved June, 2017, from http://www.investopedia.com/articles/04/111704.asphttp://money.cnn.com/retirement/guide/pensions_pensions.moneymag/index10.htm

11. Republican Party Platform Promises Social Security Privatization. (n.d.). Retrieved June, 2017, from http://www.ncpssm.org/EntitledtoKnow/entryid/2222/republican-party-platform-promises-social-security-privatization

12. Haithcock, S. G. (2014). *The Annuity Stanifesto*. Ponte Vedra Beach, FL: AnnuityMan Publishing.

13. Haithcock, S. G. (2014). *The Annuity Stanifesto*. Ponte Vedra Beach, FL: AnnuityMan Publishing.

14. Retirement Savings Annuity. (n.d.). Retrieved June, 2017, from http://money.cnn.com/2016/08/31/retirement/retirement-savings-annuity/index.html

15. Voudrie, J. D. (2008). *Why Variable Annuities Don't Work the Way You Think: Hidden Dangers That Can Devastate Retirees.*

16. Voudrie, J. D. (2008). *Why Variable Annuities Don't Work the Way You Think: Hidden Dangers That Can Devastate Retirees.*

17. Voudrie, J. D. (2008). *Why Variable Annuities Don't Work the Way You Think: Hidden Dangers That Can Devastate Retirees.*

18. Voudrie, J. D. (2008). *Why Variable Annuities Don't Work the Way You Think: Hidden Dangers That Can Devastate Retirees.*

19. Voudrie, J. D. (2008). *Why Variable Annuities Don't Work the Way You Think: Hidden Dangers That Can Devastate Retirees.*

20. Voudrie, J. D. (2008). *Why Variable Annuities Don't Work the Way You Think: Hidden Dangers That Can Devastate Retirees.*

21. Voudrie, J. D. (2008). *Why Variable Annuities Don't Work the Way You Think: Hidden Dangers That Can Devastate Retirees.*

22. Shoppers Guide to Annuity Fees. (n.d.) Retrieved June, 2017, from https://www.fidelity.com/viewpoints/retirement/shoppers-guide-to-annuity-fees

23. The Costs of Owning an Annuity. (n.d.) Retrieved June, 2017, from https://www.aaii.com/journal/article/the-costs-of-owning-an-annuity.touch

24. The Costs of Owning an Annuity. (n.d.) Retrieved June, 2017, from https://www.aaii.com/journal/article/the-costs-of-owning-an-annuity.touch

25. The Costs of Owning an Annuity. (n.d.) Retrieved June, 2017, from https://www.aaii.com/journal/article/the-costs-of-owning-an-annuity.touch

26. The Costs of Owning an Annuity. (n.d.) Retrieved June, 2017, from

https://www.aaii.com/journal/article/the-costs-of-owning-an-annuity.touch

27. How to Evaluate Annuities. (n.d.) Retrieved June, 2017, from https://www.newretirement.com/Services/Annuities_How_To_Evaluate.aspx

28. How to Assess the Financial Strength of an Insurance Company. (n.d.) Retrieved June, 2017, from http://www.iii.org/article/how-to-assess-the-financial-strength-of-an-insurance-company

29. Annuities Basics. (n.d.) Retrieved June, 2017, from http://money.cnn.com/retirement/guide/annuities_basics.moneymag/index4.htm

30. Annuities. (n.d.) Retrieved June, 2017, from http://www.investopedia.com/university/annuities/annuities2.asp

31. Annuities. (n.d.) Retrieved June, 2017, from http://www.investopedia.com/university/annuities/annuities2.asp

32. Annuities. (n.d.) Retrieved June, 2017, from http://www.investopedia.com/university/annuities/annuities2.asp

33. How 7 Different Assets Can Affect Your Financial Aid Eligibility. (n.d.). Retrieved June, 2017, from http://www.savingforcollege.com/articles/how-7-different-assets-can-affect-your-financial-aid-eligibility-716?page=6

34. The Pros and Cons of Annuities. (n.d.) Retrieved June, 2017, from https://www.fool.com/retirement/2016/01/09/the-pros-and-cons-of-annuities.aspx#main-content

35. 5 Pros and Cons of Investing in Annuities. (n.d.)
    Retrieved June, 2017, from
    http://www.bankrate.com/retirement/5-pros-and-
    cons-of-investing-in-annuities/

36. The Pros and Cons of Annuities. (n.d.). Retrieved
    June, 2017, from
    https://www.fool.com/retirement/2016/01/09/the-
    pros-and-cons-of-annuities.aspx#main-content

37. Voudrie, J. D. (2008). *Why Variable Annuities Don't
    Work the Way You Think: Hidden Dangers That Can
    Devastate Retirees.*

38. How 7 Different Assets Can Affect Your Financial Aid
    Eligibility. (n.d.). Retrieved June, 2017, from
    http://www.savingforcollege.com/articles/how-7-
    different-assets-can-affect-your-financial-aid-
    eligibility-716?page=6

39. Bill Broich Variable Annuities Secrets. (n.d.).
    Retrieved June, 2017, from
    http://www.retirevillage.com/images/Bill-Broich-
    Variable-Annuities-Secrets.pdf

40. How to Annuity Commissions Get Paid to the Agent.
    (n.d.) Retrieved June, 2017, from
    http://blog.annuity123.com/how-do-annuity-
    commissions-get-paid-to-the-agent/

41. Variable annuities trigger big paydays, red tape for
    brokers. (n.d.). retrieved June, 2017 from
    http://www.reuters.com/article/us-column-comply-
    variable-annuities-idUSBREA2Q0WE20140327

42. The Annuity 99% of clients should avoid. (n.d.).
    Retrieved June, 2017, from

http://www.thinkadvisor.com/2016/02/23/the-annuity-99-of-clients-should-avoid-and-one-tha

43. Truth About Annuities. (n.d.). Retrieved June, 2017 from http://apps.suzeorman.com/igsbase/igstemplate.cfm?SRC=MD012&SRCN=aoedetails&GnavID=20&SnavID=29&TnavID&AreasofExpertiseID=107

44. Uncovering the Mysterious Variable Annuity. (n.d.). Retrieved June, 2017, from https://www.daveramsey.com/blog/uncovering-the-mysterious-variable-annuity

45. 5 Common Mistakes When Buying a Variable Annuity. (n.d.). Retrieved June, 2017, from https://www.thestreet.com/story/11660302/2/5-common-mistakes-when-buying-a-variable-annuity.html

46. 6 Differences between Fiduciary and non-Fiduciary Advisors. (n.d.). Retrieved June, 2017, from http://blog.artifexfinancial.com/6-differences-fiduciary-vs-non-fiduciary-advisors

47. Fiduciary Registry. (n.d.). Retrieved June, 2017, from http://www.fiduciaryregistry.com/

48. Conflict of Interest Final Rule. (n.d.). Retrieved June, 2017, from https://www.dol.gov/agencies/ebsa/laws-and-regulations/rules-and-regulations/completed-rulemaking/1210-AB32-2

49. Trump Signs Executive Order Shelving Fiduciary Standard for Financial Advisors. (n.d.). Retrieved June, 2017, from https://www.forbes.com/sites/jamiehopkins/2017/02/03/trump-signs-executive-order-shelving-fiduciary-standard-for-financial-advisors/#3c4b69315863

Thank you for reading *The Truth About Annuities*. I hope that you have found the information in this book to be helpful.

My goal is to help demystify and simplify the process of figuring out the best way to plan for retirement. That said, the information contained here is necessarily incomplete. As I said before, there are thousands of different policies when it comes to Annuities and hundreds of packages. It is not possible to cover all of them here.

If there is any topic that you have questions about that I did not cover in my book, you may be able to find it at www.AnnuityMap.com

You may also want to consider calling a Financial Advisor, particularly one that is a Fiduciary. If you are uncertain about how to proceed or want additional guidance, seek help from a professional who understands annuities and how they work.

Thank you again for reading – to your continued success.

Tony J. Hansmann

Book Tony To Speak!

Book Tony Hansmann as your Keynote Speaker and You're Guaranteed to Make Your Event Memorable!

For the past 16 years Tony Hansmann has provided expert Retirement information nationwide on Television, Print, Radio and seminars.

To have Tony speak contact his booking agent at 479-268-4463.

Made in the USA
Columbia, SC
08 February 2025

52952168R10063